SASKATCHEWAN

POOL

SIMMIE

Greg McDonnell

Wheat Kings

Vanishing Landmarks of the Canadian Prairies

The BOSTON
MILLS PRESS

A BOSTON MILLS PRESS BOOK

Copyright © Greg McDonnell, 1998

NATIONAL LIBRARY OF CANADA CATALOGUING IN PUBLICATION

McDonnell, Greg, 1954-
Wheat kings : vanishing landmarks of the Canadian Prairies
/ Greg McDonnell.

ISBN 1-55046-249-0 (bound).--ISBN 1-55046-423-X (pbk.)

1. Grain elevators--Prairie Provinces--History. 2. Grain
elevators--Prairie Provinces--Pictorial works. I. Title.

TH4461.M32 1998   633.1'0468   C98-931098-1

PUBLISHER CATALOGING-IN-PUBLICATION DATA   (U.S.)

McDonnell, Greg, 1954-
Wheat kings : vanishing landmarks of the Canadian Prairies
/ Greg McDonnell.
[120] p. : col. photos. ; cm.
ISBN 1-55046-423-X (pbk.)

1. Grain elevators -- Prairie Provinces ^ Pictorial works. 2. Landscape
photography -- Prairie Provinces. I. Title.

633.1/0468 21   TR739.6.M38 2004

PUBLISHED BY BOSTON MILLS PRESS
132 Main Street, Erin, Ontario, Canada N0B 1T0
Tel 519-833-2407   Fax 519-833-2195
e-mail: books@bostonmillspress.com
www.bostonmillspress.com

IN CANADA:
Distributed by Firefly Books Ltd.
66 Leek Crescent, Richmond Hill, Ontario, Canada L4B 1H1

IN THE UNITED STATES:
Distributed by Firefly Books (U.S.) Inc.
P.O. Box 1338, Ellicott Station
Buffalo, New York, USA 14205

All photographs by the author unless otherwise noted.

MISCELLANEOUS PHOTOGRAPH IMAGES:
Jacket • Saskatchewan Wheat Pool, Killaly, Saskatchewan, May 1997
Rear Jacket • Piapot, Saskatchewan, February 1997
Page 1 • Simmie, Saskatchewan, October 1995
Page 2 • McTavish, Manitoba, August, 1997
Page 3 • Melville, Saskatchewan, May 1997
Page 5 • Hussar, Alberta, February 1997
Page 120 • Justice, Manitoba, July 1996

The publisher acknowledges for the financial support of our publishing program
the Canada Council, the Ontario Arts Council, and the Government of Canada
through the Book Publishing Industry Development Program (BPIDP).

Text and cover design by Sue Breen and Chris McCorkindale
McCorkindale Advertising & Design

Printed in Canada

ESSAYS

WHEAT KINGS

Streaming in the driveshed doorway, the hot midday sun cuts a shaft of white light through the haze of grain dust that fills the Manitoba Pool elevator at Gretna. Resident sparrows hop across the worn wooden planks that form the driveshed floor, picking at spilled grain and twittering in concert with the incessant chatter of the No. 1 loading leg. The aged wooden structure quivers and dust shakes from every seam and joint as the leg, an enclosed vertical conveyor that runs up the spine of the elevator, scoops grain from a pit beneath the floor and carries it upward.

It's the consummate prairie experience: stepping into an aging country elevator and savouring the rich aroma of new wheat and old wood; listening to the chirping birds while trading stories with the manager; watching battered old grain trucks arrive and talking bushels-per-acre, moisture content, dockage, and the politics of farming with the drivers. It's marvelling at the maze of garner levers, slides and scales, legs, cups, boots and belts—and choking back the dust as the manager puts them all into motion to move the latest load of grain from the receiving pit to storage bins. It's wood-slab walls lined with neat rows of tools, shovels and brooms, and yellowed posters that warn of the dangers of fire, spell out the specifics of boxcar and hopper loading, and shout CHILDREN NOT PERMITTED in bold print.

The country elevator is a noisy, dirty, and at times unsafe place, and yet it has an undeniable appeal. An unassuming structure designed as a facility to store and handle grain, the simple country elevator has

Manitoba Pool, Gretna, Manitoba, July 1996

eclipsed its intended role and become a prairie institution that has been woven into the social and economic fabric of the Canadian heartland. From the great elevator rows at places like Carstairs, Innisfail, Vulcan and Zealandia, to lonely granaries at unpopulated delivery points, the familiar gabled profile of the humble grain elevator has become a fixture on the prairie landscape. For more than a century, the country elevator has not

Sweeping the driveway, N. M. Paterson, Whitewood, Saskatchewan, August 1997

...the scale hopper fills with two-and-a-half tons of golden grain.

only defined the Canadian prairies, it has afforded all who care to venture inside one, a passageway to the heart and soul of prairie life.

The office door slams and the sparrows flit up into the rafters as a man in dusty coveralls and a sweat-stained ball cap crosses the driveway. He pauses at the large steel wheel that controls the distributor at the top of the No. 1 leg, rotates it to align a dust-caked arrow with the number 12, and disappears down a narrow wooden corridor that leads to the back scale.

The work floor is covered with loose grain and the wood-slab walls are thick with cobwebs and decades of dust. Long wooden garner levers reach down from the ceiling and an old Fairbanks-Morse scale reposes in front of a giant wooden hopper that receives grain from the overhead bins. The big sliding door to the outside is pushed open, but all but a few rays of daylight are obscured by a forty-foot boxcar spotted for loading.

The loading spout, a serpentine chain of bottomless buckets, reaches deep inside the empty car. CP 124047 OATS-BARLEY-FLAX-RYE-WHEAT.

The car number and load levels for various grains are stencilled on the wooden boards that line the inside of the car, and the exact profile of the previous load is clearly defined by a thick layer of dust.

In the dim yellow light of bulbs encased in explosion-proof fixtures, Ted Schmidt secures the loading spout to the top rail of the grain door that seals off the lower portion of the boxcar doorway and initiates a time-honoured ritual practised in thousands of prairie elevators for over a century. With the tug of a garner lever, the loading begins.

A deluge of grain pours from an overhead bin and a choking cloud of dust envelops the room as the scale hopper fills with two-and-a-half tons of amber grain. His face half covered by a dirty paper mask intended to make the air at least breathable, Schmidt fusses instinctively with the ancient scale and deftly manipulates the garner and hopper levers. In 4,800- to 5,100-pound portions, he carefully measures out fifty tons of No. 2 red wheat. Sampled, scaled and dropped into the pit, it is lifted by the polished-steel scoops of the leg and carried to the top of the elevator, dumped into the distributor and directed down the car spout. With a loud rush, a surging torrent of wheat, some 2,200 bushels of it, spills into the dark interior of the aging CP boxcar.

Reinforced with ribs of band iron and tension-nailed into position, the heavy cardboard grain door holds back the swelling tide of grain. An improvisation devised in the last century, the grain door handily converts a boxcar into a vehicle capable of transporting loose grain—something it was never designed to do. Grain doors have evolved from rough-hewn wood slabs nailed across the doorway, to the corrugated-paper-and-band-iron Steel-Corr doors stocked at Gretna. However, it's an invention that's had its day. The grain door market is vanishing and the art of coopering a boxcar, once practised at every elevator on the continent, is becoming a forgotten craft.

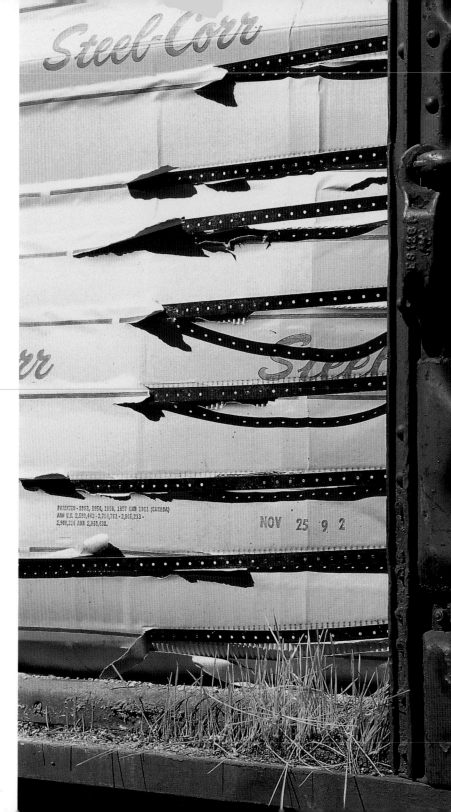

The boxcar has been a staple of the grain trade since the first sheaves of export wheat were harvested off the prairie, but in 1996, CP 124047 is a rolling anachronism. Although the Canadian grain-box fleet totalled over 20,000 cars as late as 1974, their days were numbered. By the 1980s, covered hoppers capable of carrying twice as much grain, and able to load and unload in a fraction of the time, banished the venerable grain box from all but a handful of lines unable to accommodate heavier cars. A decade later, barely a thousand grain boxes remained in service, with most of their number assigned to CN's Churchill line. Standing axle-deep in the weeds at Gretna, the 124047 and its twelve companions are among just 158 forty-foot grain boxes left in CP service.

Their rivetted flanks streaked with rust and coated with years of road dirt, the CP forty-footers wear the battle scars of more than four decades of duty like a badge of honour. Scrapes, dents and patches of fresh paint bear testament to the rigours of uncalculated millions of miles racked up wheeling prairie harvests to the Lakehead and to tidewater ports. The human touch is evidenced by grab irons polished to a shine by the grip of a thousand gloved hands, but there are biblical overtones to the tiny green shoots that sprout from germinating grain lodged in door sills and fatigue cracks in the steel sides of the cars. Scrawled in fading chalk on the side of CP 18563, a single word speaks volumes: West.

Tired coil springs creak as they slowly compress under the weight of another load and the entire carbody of CP 124047 groans in protest as the elderly car takes on fifty tons of Thunder Bay grain. Ted Schmidt scribbles the particulars of the shipment on the mandatory Canadian Grain Commission "I-90" tag that must accompany the car and staples it to the weathered placard board affixed to the car door. Car number, shipping station, date, destination, grain, grade, dockage, etc.—the I-90 documents every detail. Nowhere, though, does the government form provide for

Grain door and sprouting grain, CP 124002, Gretna, Manitoba, July 1996.

Practising the dying art of coopering a boxcar, Edwin Penner installs grain doors in CP 124002, the last car to be loaded at Gretna.

notation of the most critical information. For the 124047, and indeed for all 158 surviving CP grain boxes, this is the last harvest.

It's week fifty-two on the Wheat Board calendar, and July 31, just days away, will mark not only the end of the crop year, but the official abandonment of CP's six remaining "boxcar branches," the Dunelm, Shamrock and Neudorf subdivisions in Saskatchewan and the Lyleton, Russell and Gretna subs in Manitoba. With that, the vintage grain boxes will be out of work. Their final orders have already been issued. Upon unloading at Thunder Bay, the cars will be waybilled to Mandak in Selkirk, Manitoba, and cut up for scrap.

Seemingly oblivious to the historic occasion, Ted Schmidt labours on, loading car after car, following a procedure little changed since the Ogilvie Milling Company erected a 25,000-bushel elevator just up the track in 1881. Gretna made history when "Ogilvie's No. 8," the first standard grain elevator in western Canada, opened for business in the same year that the

CPR spiked its rails into the small village hard by the 49th parallel. One hundred fifteen years later, on July 22, 1996, Schmidt and the boys at the Pool elevator are making history of their own.

"We're closing in eight days," says manager James Borgford. Even as he speaks, Edwin Penner is preparing to install grain doors in CP 124002, the forty-foot grain box that will be the last car ever loaded in Gretna. The dilapidated elevators on the other side of the tracks haven't loaded cars in years. Ogilvie's No. 8 burned to the ground in the firestorm that ravaged Gretna on April 28, 1913, and the weather-beaten elevator that stands in its place (moved there from West Gretna in 1928) appears derelict. In a town that once boasted at least a half-dozen grain elevators, the Pool is the last active survivor. Within hours, Ted Schmidt will watch the last grains of wheat trickle into CP 124002, and as he slides the heavy steel boxcar door shut, he will also close the books on a rich chapter of prairie history. In Gretna, where it all began, the era of the country elevator has come to an end.

The situation in Gretna is far from unique. Indeed, elevator closures have been a fact of life on the prairies for decades. From a peak of 5,758 in 1933, the number of country elevators in the Prairie Provinces declined to 2,800 by 1984, and less than half that number remained by 1996. Mechanization, increased farm size, railway branchline abandonments, grain company mergers and rationalization of the grain-handling system have contributed to the demise of hundreds of country elevators, but the silo-shaped, multi-million-dollar, concrete super-elevator has sounded the death knell for the entire country elevator network on the prairies.

In ever-increasing numbers, the slip-form concrete behemoths are rising over the prairie, and each one of the new-generation facilities spells doom for dozens of small-town elevators. Called "high-throughput grain-handling centres" in corporate parlance, the super-elevators boast capacities nearly ten times greater than that of the average country elevator. And, while Ted Schmidt can fill a boxcar with 2,200 bushels of wheat in fifteen to twenty minutes, the new state-of-the-art elevators can disgorge 30,000 bushels an hour and spot 50 to 100 covered hoppers at a time.

It's impossible to dispute the efficiencies of the new order, but the cost can be measured in more than the splintered wreckage of abandoned elevators scattered across the prairie. Closed cafes, boarded-up storefronts and virtual ghost towns are becoming commonplace as the fortunes of countless small communities follow that of the country elevators and railway lines that spawned them.

As the twentieth century comes to a close, the classic wooden elevators that have become intrinsic to the very identity of the Canadian Prairies are tumbling like dominoes in the wake of the super-elevator and the globalization of the grain trade. With an ambition morbidly similar to that of the construction crews that in the early part of the century moved from place to place building elevators, demolition contractors are plying their trade across the prairie. "On a quiet day in Calgary," muses historian Doug Phillips, "you can hear the sound of elevators crashing down in the country." As each one falls, the prairie becomes a lonelier place.

Framed in the doorway of CP 124002, Manitoba Pool, Gretna, Manitoba, July 1996.

Hussar, Alberta, February 1997

Hussar, Alberta, February 1997

Rosetown, Saskatchewan, February 1988

Andrew J. Sutherland

Craigmyle, Alberta, February 1997

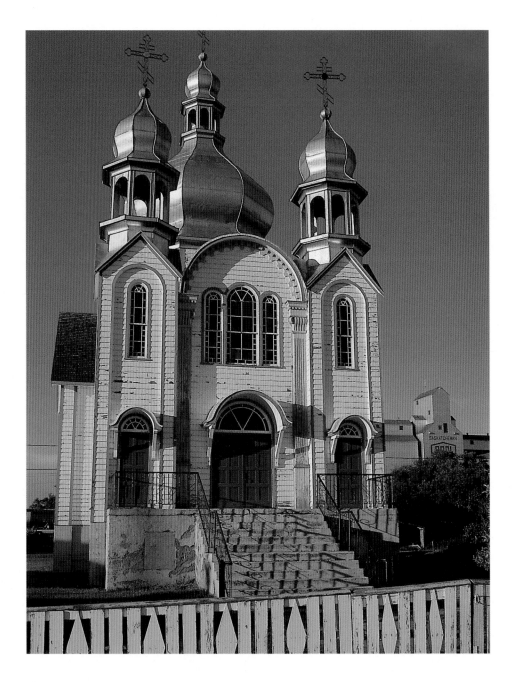

Prairie Cathedrals: Greek Orthodox Church of St. Elia
and Saskatchewan Wheat Pool Wroxton A,
Wroxton, Saskatchewan, July 1996

Quill Lake, Saskatchewan, May 1997

Marchwell, Saskatchewan, September 1970

James A. Brown

Sixteen-hundreds, CN Lewvan Subdivision, Saskatchewan, September 1997

Tom Lambrecht

Brooks, Alberta, October 1995

Strasbourg, Saskatchewan, July 1996

McTavish, Manitoba, August 1997

Domain, Manitoba, August 1997

Edgeley, Saskatchewan, May 1997

Frank Malach unloading oats at Saskatchewan Wheat Pool, Edgeley, Saskatchewan, May 1997.

Sifton, Manitoba, May 1992

Mark Perry

Fleming, Saskatchewan, June 1997

Mark Perry

Whitewood, Saskatchewan, August 1997

Duck Lake, Saskatchewan, January 1987
Andrew J. Sutherland

Didsbury, Alberta, February 1997

Gull Lake, Saskatchewan, October 1995

Saskatchewan Wheat Pool, Gull Lake B, Gull Lake, Saskatchewan, October 1995

Framed in Canadian Northern roundhouse ruins,
Alberta Wheat Pool, Big Valley, Alberta, February 1997.

Saskatchewan Pool No. 1, Bulyea, Saskatchewan, July 1996

MacNutt, Saskatchewan, July 1996

Manitoba Pool Dauphin C, Dauphin, Manitoba August 1991

Mark Perry

Neepawa, Manitoba, July 1980

Mortlach, Saskatchewan, September 1997

A. Ross Harrison

Secrets revealed, Boissevain, Manitoba, June 1997

A. Ross Harrison

Bin chart, Saskatchewan Wheat Pool Gull Lake B, Gull Lake, Saskatchewan, October 1995

Dacotah, Manitoba, August 1997

Harvest moon, N.M. Paterson, Dacotah, Manitoba, September 1994

A. Ross Harrison

Maryfield, Saskatchewan, August 1997

Studebaker and Saskatchewan Wheat Pool, Webb, Saskatchewan, October 1995

Edgeley, Saskatchewan, May 1997

United Grain Growers, Swan Lake, Manitoba, August 1997

James Weiler measures out a boxcar-load of No. 2 red wheat at Saskatchewan Wheat Pool, McMahon, Saskatchewan, October 1995.

Grain samples and the ever-present Edwards Coffee can, Saskatchewan Wheat Pool, McMahon, Saskatchewan, October 1995.

McMahon, Saskatchewan, October 1995

James Weiler, Saskatchewan Wheat Pool, McMahon, Saskatchewan,
October 1995

Pioneer Grain, McMahon, Saskatchewan, October 1995

Glen Slimmon, agent, N.M. Paterson, Cracknell, Manitoba, June 1997

Mark Perry

Vern Hiebert loading CNWX 111493, Saskatchewan
Wheat Pool Zelma, Saskatchewan, May 1997.

Reston, Manitoba, May 1997

Stony Beach, Saskatchewan, August 1997

Bow Island, Alberta, September 1995

A. Ross Harrison

Moonrise, Ituna, Saskatchewan, July 1996

OF PEDDLERS, PULLERS AND TRAMPS

Keep the Crow. The faded graffiti on the side of a government grain car sends a poignant message as the short train rolls into Wroxton, Saskatchewan, at sunset. The three-word slogan is the legacy of a campaign waged to save the Crowsnest Pass Agreement, a federal decree that had kept a lid on grain transportation rates since 1897. From a prairie perspective, "the Crow" was perhaps the most sacrosanct legislation passed since Confederation, and contingents of western farmers fought hard to keep it alive. Alas, the pleas from the Prairie fell on deaf ears in Ottawa, and on August 1, 1995, the last vestiges of the Crow Agreement were struck down. A year later, as CNWX 395744 rolls into town wearing the ill-fated slogan, Wroxton is about to suffer the consequences of the Crow's demise.

It hung like an albatross around the necks of the railroad companies for ninety-eight years, but the Crow helped preserve not only country elevators and prairie branchlines, but hundreds of communities that had grown up around the railway and lineside elevators. With a station at the foot of Main Street and a row of elevators along Railway Avenue, they were strung like beads on the rail lines that crossed the prairie. They could survive the loss of their passenger trains and the demolition of the station at the end of Main Street, just as long as the wayfreight that worked the line kept calling on the elevators to spot empties and pull loads.

Sustained by the Crow, and the Crow Rate Benefit that compensated railways for their losses, the peddlers, pullers and tramps that patrolled the back-country branches and elevator tracks were the lifeblood of the country elevator system. In Amaranth, Elgin and Irricana, Simmie, Snowflake, Swan Lake and countless other prairie points, the lonesome call of a whistle in the night, the sound of steel wheels squealing through the turnouts on the back track, or just the sight of a string of empties spotted at the elevator meant the world was right.

"Keep the Crow" CNWX 395744

The world seems right as CN GMD1's 1606 and 1600 spot a cut of empty grain hoppers at Sask Pool's Wroxton A on July 21, 1996.

Wroxton, Saskatchewan, July 1997

Mark Perry

The world seems right as CN GMD1's 1606 and 1600 spot a cut of empty grain hoppers at Sask Pool's Wroxton A on July 21, 1996—but it won't be for long. Wroxton, population 49, has seen better days. The John Deere dealership, the Co-Op gas station, and the hardware and grocery stores are gone. Sask Pool's Wroxton A is all that remains of the row of elevators that once lined the tracks, and Tataryn's General Store is the last store in business on the dusty, unnamed streets of the sleepy village. Way-freights have been working the elevator tracks here since the Canadian

Northern came to town in 1911. However, only three more trains will call on Wroxton.

In the post-Crow era of branchline rationalization, super-elevators and "economies of scale," Wroxton's sole surviving elevator is being forced to close and its rail line, CN's Rhein Subdivision, abandoned. By the following summer, the rails through Wroxton will be ripped up and Wroxton A will be boarded shut, the old lady at Tataryn's will be talking about closing up shop, and another prairie town will be one step closer to oblivion.

CN No. 553, MacNutt, Saskatchewan, July 1996

CP Bassano Wayfreight, Hussar, Alberta, February 1997

CP No. 86, Hagen, Saskatchewan, November 1980

Andrew J. Sutherland

CN Amaranth Wayfreight, Longburn, Manitoba, July 1980

Sunrise at Simmie, Saskatchewan, July 1996

Mark Perry

McMahon, Saskatchewan, October 1995

Dauphin, Manitoba, November 1996

Mark Perry

CPWX 608261

CPWX 605752

CP 21951

CP 18563

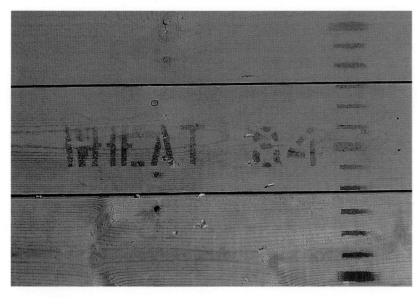

CP 124002

CN 446573

CN 445209

CP 21861

CP "Weyburn Tramp," Ceylon, Saskatchewan, June 1997

A. Ross Harrison

CP Matador Wayfreight, Sanctuary, Saskatchewan, August 1977

Andrew J. Sutherland

CP La Riviere Sub Wayfreight, west of Rosenfeld, Manitoba, August 1984

CP "Regina Tramp," east of Francis, Saskatchewan, June 1997

A. Ross Harrison

Lipton, Saskatchewan, July 1996

CP "Regina Tramp," Lipton, Saskatchewan, July 1996

CN No. 834, Lowe Farm, Manitoba, July 1980

CN No. 572, Estlin, Saskatchewan, August 1997

CP "Weyburn Tramp," Radville, Saskatchewan, June 1997

A. Ross Harrison

CP "Assiniboia Tramp," Rockglen, Saskatchewan, June 1997

A. Ross Harrison

For D. P. M., CN 1027, Margaret, Manitoba,
August 1984

Relics, Morris, Manitoba, July 1980

Napinka Sub Wayfreight, Clearwater, Manitoba, September 1976

Andrew Sutherland

CP "Assiniboia Tramp," Rock Glen, Saskatchewan, September 1997

Tom Lambrecht

Saskatchewan Wheat Pool, McMahon, Saskatchewan, October 1995

Door seals, Saskatchewan Wheat Pool, McMahon, Saskatchewan, October 1995

Hudson Bay, Saskatchewan, July 1994

Tom Lambrecht

SOMETHING BIG ON THE HORIZON

For eighty-five years, the Saskatchewan Pool elevator at Fairlight has towered above the prairie like a boxcar-red beacon. Bleached by the hot summer sun and buffeted by the ever-present wind, it has endured drought and depression and withstood the scrutiny of sharp-pencilled auditors always looking to eliminate under-utilized elevators.

Erected beside the CPR Reston Subdivision in 1912, the 45,000-bushel elevator was passed from the Saskatchewan Co-op Elevator Company to the newly formed Saskatchewan Wheat Pool in 1926. CP abandoned the Reston Sub in 1961, but Pool elevator No. 222 escaped the demolition crews and was moved to the outskirts of town, where it joined the Federal elevator on the CN Cromer Subdivision. The neighbouring elevators became Sask Pool Fairlight A and B in 1972, after the Manitoba, Saskatchewan and Alberta pools purchased the facilities of the Federal Grain Company in their home provinces. Several years later, the former Federal elevator was sold and moved, while its 40,000-bushel crib annex was relocated beside the Fairlight A.

Generations of farmers have hauled their grain to the old Fairlight elevator. In horse-drawn wagons, sputtering Model A's and turbocharged semis, they've come to "the Pool" for more than a grain ticket or a supply of fertilizer. Like almost every other elevator on the face of the prairie, Fairlight has been a place to hear the news—news of births and deaths and war and peace. It's been a place to debate politics, wheat prices, wheat boards and hockey; a place to shake the loneliness of life on the land. On a hot summer afternoon, there was the shade of the driveway. In the depths of winter, there was the warmth of the office, with worn wooden chairs and a pot of coffee to pass the time while the howling wind shook the driveway doors, the snow drifted high and the mercury in the thermometer plunged out of sight.

"Something Big on the Horizon." The ominous-sounding words on Sask Pool billboards confirmed rumours of a super-elevator to be built near Fairlight. In the winter of '97, cranes and concrete forms climbed slowly over the western horizon as contractors poured 6,900 cubic yards of cement and $8.5 million into the futuristic-looking facility taking shape in the distance. By August, it was done.

Christened "8-48 Crossroads" by owner Saskatchewan Pool, the new high-throughput facility dwarfed the 2,240-ton-capacity elevator at Fairlight in stature and statistics. Boasting a total storage capacity of 26,300 tons, as well as the capability to dry 50 tons of grain per hour and clean 120 tons in the same time, 8-48 Crossroads surely spelled doom for the Fairlight landmark.

Not so. SWP No. 222's luck hadn't run out yet, and fate intervened once more. Instead of putting out a demolition contract on the ancient elevator, Sask Pool pressed the 1912-vintage structure into service as a satellite facility of the new 8-48, employing it for the storage of low-volume stocks of specialty grains.

For the moment, the past and the future share space on the vast Saskatchewan skyline at Fairlight, and for at least a little while longer, the 85-year-old elevator will remain something big on the horizon.

Fairlight, Saskatchewan, August 1997

McMahon—Hard Times on the Prairie

In the pre-dawn gloom of an overcast February morning, McMahon, Saskatchewan, has the look and feel of a ghost town. A bone-chilling wind whips through an abandoned homestead, swirling snow around derelict buildings and piling drifts against the bulbous nose of a rusting, fifty-year-old panel truck. The loading spouts of the Sask Pool elevator gently sway and the old building creaks eerily as the wind picks at its metal-clad walls and pounds in vain on the locked driveway doors. The streets are deserted, and but for the lights burning in the windows of the drab grey building labelled CO-OP in blistered white letters, there is little evidence of life.

Since the elevators closed last summer, the dilapidated Co-Op is pretty much the heart of McMahon. From the cases of Libby's beans and boxes of Weyerhauser computer paper piled together on the floor, to the air filters stocked next to the chocolate bars; from the array of fanbelts hanging from ceiling-height hooks, to the crokinole board leaned up against the potato-chip stand, the McMahon Co-Op is the quintessential country store.

"Everybody thinks we're closing," says Colleen Gillespie from behind the counter, "but we're *not*." There's coffee brewing and freshly baked muffins on the table, but business is slow on this miserable morning. Only six people live in the tiny Saskatchewan village named, it's said, in honour of a CPR brakeman from Smiths Falls, Ontario. Even the CPR doesn't come here anymore.

McMahon's two elevators closed shortly after the last CP train left town in the summer of 1996. Locked up tight, the Pool awaits the inevitable arrival of the wreckers; the Pioneer met its end in December. "The demo-

Colleen Gillespie, McMahon Co-Op, McMahon, Saskatchewan, February 1997

lition contractor came here the day before to set up," recalls Gillespie. He'd done forty-seven elevators that year. On the appointed day, the streets of McMahon were lined with people. "Everybody came to watch," she says. "They tore it down and burned it. I thought it was sad."

With the elevators gone and the railway line abandoned, it will be difficult for McMahon to survive. If Colleen Gillespie has her way, though, the lights of the McMahon Co-Op will greet the prairie dawn for years to come.

McMahon, Saskatchewan, February 1997

THE LAST HARVEST

Drifting on the wind, the song of a meadowlark carries across the prairie on a May afternoon. The dull brown and lifeless grey remnants of the Saskatchewan winterscape steadily submit to the rich greens of spring as nature wrestles away winter's grip on the land. The tilled soil clutches the seed of a new season's crop and the warmth of the sun coaxes new life from the earth. Bearing silent witness to the miracle of spring, the old elevator at Lewvan stands ready to receive the fruits of a new harvest, just as it has for nearly ninety years.

Without warning, a diesel engine roars to life, silencing the meadowlark and propelling a large yellow backhoe in the direction of the elevator. Flexing its hydraulic muscle, the powerful machine claws at the base of the structure with its shovel. Ancient timbers splinter and break as the shovel tears away at the six-inch-thick wooden walls.

Working the machine like an extension of his own arms, demolition contractor Ray Velos methodically carves a deep gash in the base of the bright-red Pioneer elevator, then nudges the boom against the building to push it over. Once, twice, three times; the big machine struggles in vain to knock the elevator down. Heavy steel treads churn the rich black soil and the diesel engine roars angrily, but the aging elevator stands fast. The machine backs off in defeat.

Climbing down from the backhoe, Velos looks over at the still-standing elevator in frustration. "I chewed away at the corner with the Case, but the

Ken Aasen, Lewvan, Saskatchewan, May 1997

Lewvan, Saskatchewan, May 1997

Pioneer Lewvan meets its end, Lewvan, Saskatchewan, May 1997

son of a bitch wouldn't go over." He fires up a John Deere bulldozer and heads back into the fray.

From behind the annex, the Deere goes at the ravaged elevator with a vengeance. The sounds of violence, the snapping of timbers and the snarling of the Deere are unsettling. In a moment it's over. With an anguished groan and a gut-wrenching crash, the venerable structure topples, hitting the ground in a massive eruption of nine decades of dust. The Lewvan Pioneer has seen its last harvest.

Wearing a dusty black cap embroidered "The Pioneer, Lewvan, Sask.," Ken Aasen surveys the wreckage in silence. "That's it," he says, and walks away. The meadowlark resumes its song and the seeds of the next harvest slowly push their way through the soil.

Lewvan, Saskatchewan, May 1997

Maples Co-Operative Elevator Association No. 129, Virden, Saskatchewan, August 1997

Runneymede, Saskatchewan, November 1997

Mark Perry

Saskatchewan Wheat Pool Neelby A, Neelby, Saskatchewan, August 1997

Mark Perry

Canada's last row, Inglis, Manitoba, October 1996

Mark Perry

Rowley, Alberta, February 1997

Piapot, Saskatchewan, February 1997

Barnsley, Manitoba, July 1996

Saskatchewan Wheat Pool, Bender, Saskatchewan, August 1997

Duchess, Alberta, October 1995

Duchess, Alberta, October 1995

Saskatchewan Wheat Pool, Bender, Saskatchewan, August 1997

Elevator engine, Saskatchewan Wheat Pool,
Bender, Saskatchewan, August 1997

Saskatchewan Wheat Pool, Walpole, Saskatchewan, August 1997

Avonhurst, Saskatchewan, May 1997

Grain wagon, Dunelm, Saskatchewan, October 1995

Ex-CP 95534, Gleichen, Alberta, October 1995

Ex-CP 96558, Gleichen, Alberta, October 1995

Saskatchewan Wheat Pool and wreckage of Pioneer Grain elevator,
Simmie, Saskatchewan, February 1997

McDowell, Saskatchewan, January 1987

Andrew J. Sutherland

Mikado, Saskatchewan, November 1997

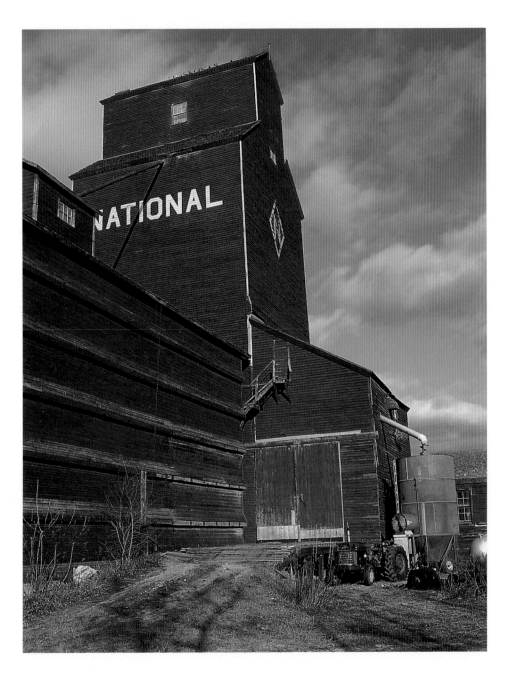

Winnipegosis, Manitoba, November 1996

Mark Perry

Saskatchewan Wheat Pool, Neelby A and B, Neelby, Saskatchewan, August 1997

Saskatchewan Wheat Pool, Bender, Saskatchewan, August 1997

Manitoba Pool No. 40, Lenore, Manitoba, September 1997

Mark Perry

Killaly, Saskatchewan, July 1996

BUFFALO BONES

Battered, broken and stripped of their trucks, several hundred CN forty-foot grain boxes languish in a muddy scrapyard on the outskirts of Selkirk, Manitoba. The scene recalls disturbing images from history books and old glass-plate negatives of enormous stacks of buffalo bones piled on the prairie. Ironically, the rivetted flanks of every car are emblazoned with a stencilled outline of Manitoba's provincial symbol, the buffalo.

The distinctive marking gave CN's "Buffalo" boxes their name, but the 900 forty-foot boxcars rehabilitated with federal and provincial funds gained greater recognition as the last great fleet of grain boxes on the continent. Although covered hoppers had forced the grain box to near extinction almost everywhere else, the Buffalos survived due to their ability to tread where 100-ton hoppers were forbidden to go—specifically, over the soggy muskeg and frozen tundra, to the Arctic tidewater at Churchill. To that end, the CN forty-footers bore not only the logos of their federal and provincial sponsors, but they were stencilled with a strict proviso: "This car not to be interchanged—for Churchill & Thunder Bay grain service only."

In spring and summer, the famed Buffalos took on loads of Churchill grain at elevators in Manitoba and eastern Saskatchewan, and moved to the Arctic port in impressive 165-car trains. In the winter months, they earned their keep hauling grain to the Lakehead and discharging their burden at Saskatchewan Pool's mammoth 7A terminal elevator in Thunder Bay. Elevator workers and railroaders alike cursed the road-weary cars, but they were the lifeline that kept the controversial Hudson Bay port of Churchill alive.

Just prior to selling the Hudson Bay line to shortline operator Omnitrax, CN lifted the ban on grain hoppers in late 1996. Good news for Churchill, bad news for Buffalos. On December 5th of the same year, the very last train of loaded Buffalos departed Canora, Saskatchewan, with seventy-four loads of Thunder Bay grain and forty cars of grain screenings from Churchill. The era of the grain box had ended. Except for a handful of cars retained for company service, the Buffalos were rounded up and herded, by the hundreds, to the boneyard in Selkirk.

There's no room for sentiment in the crowded Selkirk scrapyard. In the eyes of those who work there, the Buffalos are just so much steel and aluminium to be shredded and sorted for recycling. For mobile shear operator Richard Swiderski, every Buffalo box in the yard means little more than twenty minutes of work.

Around the yard, they call Swiderski's machine "the chicken," but the Liebherr 974 backhoe, with its pincer-like fifty-ton hydraulic shear, is a fearsome piece of equipment. With remarkable precision, Swiderski carefully sinks the machine's claw into CN 445572 and peels off the aluminium roof like a tinfoil wrapper, then flips the car on its back, snips the frame and cuts it in two. Effortlessly, the machine grabs each half of the dismembered car and shakes it, dislodging the hardwood tongue-and-groove flooring. Then, with a rapid succession of precise cuts, Swiderski slices the Buffalo to pieces. In just twenty-two minutes, the procedure is over and Swiderski moves on, leaving the broken remains of the 445572 lying in the mud like buffalo bones on the prairie. Following the fate of the great herds of buffalo that once roamed the land, the grain box, too, has all but vanished.

Selkirk, Manitoba, May 1997

WHEAT KINGS (REPRISE)

Licence to Operate a Public Country Elevator. To whom it may concern, The license Fee of Five Dollars having been paid and the necessary security filed with the Board of Grain Commissioners of Canada SASKATCHEWAN WHEAT POOL of REGINA, SASKATCHEWAN is hereby licensed to operate a Public Country Elevator at NEELBY B SASKATCHEWAN as described in its application, in accordance with the terms and conditions thereof, the provisions of the Canada Grain Act, and amendments thereto, and the regulations and orders of the Board of Grain Commissioners for Canada. ...Issued at Winnipeg, Manitoba, this FIRST day of AUGUST 1957.

J. Laird, Issuing Officer

Forty years after J. Laird signed and sealed the grain commissioner's license, it remains stapled to the wall of the Neelby B elevator. Sask Pool abandoned and sold the Neelby A and B elevators decades ago, and the CPR line through Neelby was torn out in the fall of 1961. Listing noticeably, the neighbouring Neelby A elevator stands abandoned. Neelby B, however, remains intact and operable, as if suspended in time.

The years have faded the Saskatchewan Pool paint on its metal-clad exterior, revealing the Federal Grain Ltd. lettering of its earlier owner, and the wind has torn away sections of tin sheathing to expose rotted wood and cribwork. Still, Neelby B is a throwback right down to the Ruston & Hornsby "Mark CY Canadian Elevator Engine" secreted in the rust-streaked engine shed.

Neelby B, Neelby, Saskatchewan, August 1997

Saskatchewan Wheat Pool, Neelby B, Neelby, Saskatchewan, August 1997

Leonard Richmond, the 84-year-old farmer whose chores include tending to the privately owned elevator, carefully positions the large flywheel of the Mark CY, lights a saltpetre fuse and threads it into the combustion chamber of the aging engine. With a muffled shot, the single-cylinder

Leonard Richmond and Ruston & Hornsby elevator engine, Neelby B, Neelby, Saskatchewan, August 1997

Leonard Richmond, Neelby B, Neelby, Saskatchewan, August 1997

diesel comes to life. The flywheel whirs madly, driving a system of leather belts that operate the elevator, and the years fall away.

To the rapid beat of the Mark CY and the slapping sound of leather belt-drives, Neelby B awakens, conjuring visions of farmers arriving with wheat piled high in horse-drawn wagons and Model A trucks, of workers in peaked caps and dungarees, and of rivers of grain spilling into wooden boxcars. For a brief moment, the past is present.

The sky is dark and the thunder of an approaching storm rolls across the prairie as Leonard locks the doors of Neelby B. "The doctor tells me I won't last long if I quit," he says. Quitting, however, is not in his plans. The first drops of rain spatter the ground as Leonard climbs into his old Ford pick-up and heads home for the day. As long as he keeps returning, Leonard and Neelby B will be part of a precious link with the tradition and heritage of the prairie and the nation—the tradition and heritage of the Wheat Kings.

Saskatchewan Wheat Pool, Neelby B, Neelby, Saskatchewan, August 1997